Southern Rooms II

Southern Rooms II

THE TIMELESS BEAUTY *of the* AMERICAN SOUTH

GLOUCESTER MASSACHUSETTS

QUARRY BOOKS

SHANNON HOWARD

First published in the United States of America by
Quarry Books, a member of
Quayside Publishing Group
33 Commercial Street
Gloucester, Massachusetts 01930-5089
Telephone: (978) 282-9590
Fax: (978) 283-2742
www.rockpub.com

Library of Congress Cataloging-in-Publication Data
Howard, Shannon.
    Southern rooms II: the timeless beauty of the American South /
Shannon Howard.
            p.   cm.
    I. Interior decoration—Southern States. I. Title: Southern rooms 2
    II. Title.
NK2006.H69 2005
747'.0975—dc22   2004028911
                                                         CIP

ISBN 1-59253-160-1

10 9 8 7 6 5 4 3 2

Cover Design: Mary Ann Guillette
Design: John Hall Design Group   www.johnhalldesign.com
Cover Image: Brian Vandenbrink/Group 3 Architecture Interiors
    Planning
Back Cover Images: Courtesy of Ethan Allen, right
    Suzanne Kasler/William Waldron, all others

Contents

Introduction

Visit the South, if only for a short while, and you'll discover an enchanting place of profound intensity. Still heavy with time and painted with the faded grandeur of history, it is a land that lingers on its own terms and quietly seduces all who fall captive to its charms. From the back-road bayous of Louisiana, where cypress knees peek through cloudy swamps, to the lush green hills of Tennessee, where ghosts of moonshiners and music legends rise up through the haze, the South abounds with unparalleled beauty.

Across every inch of the landscape, in both blue-blood cities and idyllic countrysides, the aura of this loveliness is remarkably far-reaching. You can hear it in the gentle lilt of a Southern accent or the rolling melodies of Dixieland jazz. You can feel it in the firm grasp of a Southern gentleman, who still marks his word with a handshake, not a pen. And you can certainly see it—this essence of Southern style—in the unique and often haunting architecture for which this region is so beloved.

Steeped in such elegance and allure, it's no wonder that the South has inspired so many. Artists and authors, filmmakers and poets—all have plumbed the tales and trials of this land. And throughout America, even throughout the globe, the influence of the South is undeniable. Far beyond Antietam and *Gone with the Wind*, which still endure in the minds of many, perhaps the greatest mark made by modern Southerners can be seen in the world of interior design.

No matter where you go in the South, from the storied streets of Birmingham to the wide-open skies of Texas, you will always find a gracious host and an open door. Home is sacred to the Southerner, a place to welcome guests, cherish family, celebrate beauty, and pass the time. And so it makes sense that designing a home—crafting it to reflect the heart and soul of its owner—would be a treasured pursuit in this corner of the country.

Of all the Southern cities, Atlanta is most renowned for great design. But throughout the South, you'll find countless talented designers exploring a wide variety of styles and trends. The look is no longer just fainting couches and curtains that evoke the rooms of Tara. Instead, the South is alive with eclectic spirit, rustic warmth, and modern finesse. And as ever, it embraces the mel-

low feel of a casual family home and the time-touched splendor of traditional refinement.

These divergent paths, all uniquely Southern, are what you'll find in *Southern Rooms II*. Gracious, radiant spaces. Relaxed and inviting living areas. Lighthearted rooms with a quirky sense of style. Featuring many of the South's most well known designers, as well as some rising stars whose names you may not know, this book visits grand mansions, humble abodes, historic plantations, and some of the most delightful and inspiring homes you'll ever see.

It is a testament to yesteryear and an invitation to join in the fun today. So come in, enjoy, and lose yourself in the timeless beauty of the American South.

ABOVE: The beauty of the South is crafted from a wide range of influences. In this winsome Florida home, designer Rod Mickley mingled seaside charm with a hint of European glamour.

OPPOSITE: For Atlanta designer Suzanne Kasler, the key to achieving traditional Southern style is to approach it in a very non-traditional way. "Give it a twist," she likes to say. And that's exactly what she did in this sun-washed dining room, in which contemporary furniture fuses gracefully with classical architecture.

Exploring Southern Style

Southern
Roots

"In the South, the breeze blows softer...
neighbors are friendlier, nosier, and more talkative. This is a different place.
Our way of thinking is different, as are our ways of seeing, laughing, singing,
eating, meeting, and parting. What we carry in our memories is different too,
and that may explain everything else."

That's what the great storyteller Charles Kuralt once said of his beloved
homeland, and it's an apt metaphor for the unique experiences that have
shaped Southern life and indeed, Southern style. At its heart, the South is
a vast patchwork of cultures, each woven into the larger identity through
the shared joys and sorrows of history. And each culture, in its own way,
has stained this region with vibrant flavors and unique charms that still
resonate today.

When it comes to Southern design, the roots run deeply in three direc-
tions: Colonial, Romantic, and Victorian. Each of these architectural styles rose
to prominence in the South, shaping not just the appearance of homes and
buildings but also the way that people lived and how they viewed the world.
Though the needs and philosophies that inspired each style have long since
evolved, their effects can still be seen today.

**A grand *allée* of twenty-eight live oaks cradles the entranceway of Bon
Sejour, the Louisiana plantation better known as Oak Alley. Planted in the
early 1700s by a French settler, the trees actually predate the stately Greek
Revival house by more than a century.**

Colonial

Travel anywhere in the South—in fact, almost anywhere in the United States—and you're bound to see examples of colonial architecture. Practical, straightforward, and highly personal, it reflects the building traditions of early settlers, who adapted the aesthetic conventions of their native countries to suit the local climate and landscape. Though colonial homes are often associated with stately, symmetrical façades and orderly arrangements of windows, in reality, they take many different forms.

One of the most distinctive varieties seen in the South is **French Creole** architecture, which rose to prominence at the beginning of the eighteenth century. Rare jewels located primarily around the Mississippi delta region, French Creole houses (especially in rural areas) are remarkable for their steeply pitched roofs, heavy timber frames, and broad porches. They're generally asymmetrical with no interior hallways, and they often have irregular groupings of doors and windows on the exterior.

In the days before air-conditioning, Creoles built foundations on top of brick pillars or piles, allowing air to circulate from below. In urban areas, where they favored townhouses and cottages instead of plantation-sized structures, many Creole families fashioned their homes around a rear courtyard, which afforded a private space for tasks like cooking, washing, and raising chickens.

More rustic but just as casual and welcoming as French Creole architecture is **Spanish Colonial,** a type of building seen throughout Texas, Florida, and parts of the Gulf Coast. Dating from about 1600 to 1850, homes of this style feature flat

or low-pitched roofs, thick adobe walls, and a long, covered front porch. Because some have imposing gated entrances and few windows, Spanish Colonial houses may look like fortresses from the outside. But step inside and you'll find gently meandering living spaces centered on a lush courtyard.

Relaxed and relatively unadorned, Spanish Colonial architecture relies on the subtle beauty of natural materials and the honest elegance of handcrafted shapes and details. A typical *casa,* built to host family gatherings and provide a temperate retreat from harsh weather, has curved archways between rooms and ornamentation only on doors and windows.

ABOVE RIGHT: Though its grandeur has faded a bit over the years, the 1817 Aiken-Rhett house in Charleston offers a compelling glimpse at high-society life in the nineteenth century.

OPPOSITE: Reminiscent of architectural motifs from ancient Greece and Rome, these heavily carved moldings and acanthus leaf rosettes are characteristic of a Federal style home.

In sharp contrast, eighteenth- and nineteenth-century **Federal**-style homes were much more ornate. Remarkable for their curved lines and decorative flourishes, these regal dwellings were inspired by the ancient temples of Rome and Greece, and often had rounded-top windows and a half-moon fanlight over the front door. Sometimes called "Adamesque," in honor of two British brothers who founded the movement, Federalist architecture descended directly from **Georgian Colonial**, the most popular American building style of the 1700s.

Seen widely throughout the Southeast (and elsewhere), Georgian homes reveal the importance of order and civility during this era, as well as the classical influence of sixteenth-century Italian architect Andrea Palladio. Formal, boxy, and strictly symmetrical, they often boast grand pediments and pilasters, fancy masonry, and an orderly row of five windows across the second story. The layout revolves around a central hall, usually with fireplaces on either end of the house, and carved moldings are used both inside and out. Today, modern Georgians are popular in every corner of the country, especially in the South, where they're prized for their dignified appearance and traditional sensibility.

Romantic

No discussion of Southern architecture would be complete without mentioning two of the region's most famous houses—both of which, not by accident, are "Romantic" in style. Thomas Jefferson's Monticello, perhaps the most well known building below the Mason-Dixon, was designed in 1769 to reflect ancient Roman ideals of beauty and proportion. Graced with a glorious domed roofline, multiple skylights, and several octagonal rooms, Monticello is a unique example of **Roman Neoclassical** architecture.

Tara, the South's second most celebrated home, is actually not a home at all, but rather a stage set created for *Gone with the Wind*. With elements inspired by genuine Southern houses (including a staircase from Chretien Point Plantation in Louisiana), the genteel "mansion" is quintessentially **Greek Revival**. Sharing many of the same features as Monticello, including classical detailing and massive scale, Tara is best remembered for its towering Doric columns and sweeping verandas. Like most Greek Revival homes built between 1820 and 1850, it also has a low-pitched roof, heavy cornices, and bold, elaborate moldings.

Once called the "National Style" because of its incredible popularity, Greek Revival was used for everything from banks and federal buildings to townhomes and farmhouses. Somewhat stiff and austere, it eventually gave way to less restrained Victorian styles.

ABOVE RIGHT: Housed in an 1825 *garçonniere*, this modern "Creole family altar" is lovingly festooned with treasures from the past. The portrait of Charlotte Mathilde Grevemberg du Martait was painted posthumously in 1843.

OPPOSITE: This humble bedroom at Louisiana's Laura Plantation offered a restful retreat for the women of the family. The men at Laura slept in another parlor, following a Creole tradition wherein males live in the down-river side of the house and women in the up river.

Victorian

For a brief period following the Civil War (about 1880-1910), the clean lines and inherent simplicity of antebellum architecture were no longer in vogue. In burgeoning Southern cities like Savannah and Charleston, the style of choice became Victorian, a purely American concoction marked by asymmetrical layouts, intricate gingerbread trim, and vivid colors.

ABOVE: Guests were often entertained in this ornate parlor at the Aiken-Rhett house. The large portrait shows Harriet Lowndes, wife of William Aiken Jr. and one of Charleston's most gracious nineteenth-century hostesses.

OPPOSITE: Though built in 1856, the San Francisco Plantation in Louisiana is certainly not a typical pre-war home. With its brilliant colors, varied patterns, and extensive hand-painted detailing, it could almost pass as a Victorian.

Queen Anne became the most prevalent variety of Victorian home, easily distinguishable by its textured shingles and dominant front-facing gable. Wildly eclectic and somewhat busy, it was a favorite of the urban upper classes, who were drawn to its ostentatious flair. In more rural areas, **Gothic Revival** was preferred, with both houses and churches bearing its steeply pitched roofs and fanciful trimwork. And though much of the country embraced **Italianate** architecture, it never really took hold in the South, as its popularity peaked at the height of the Civil War.

Southerners were also slow to adopt the **Arts and Crafts** movement and most of the modern architectural styles that followed. Except for Florida, which blossomed with a vast number of **Art Deco** masterpieces, few Southern states led the way when it came to modernism—a fact that seems perfectly reasonable in a land so rich with history.

Traditional design evokes
the grand style and demure
elegance of the past. Precise
and classical, with regal details
that hint at quiet strength, it
is keenly proportioned yet
invitingly warm.

Traditional

Rather than upholster these chairs in a solid rose-toned fabric, designer Suzanne Kasler opted for a more subtle approach by adding a vivid blush-colored flange where the skirt meets the floor.

> "Southerners demonstrate a distinct sensitivity to design. You can see it in their love of fine things, beautiful architecture, and exceptional antiques."

SUZANNE KASLER

A Fresh Take on
Formal

Some people believe that historical homes should go hand in hand with period furnishings, but not the owners of this Atlanta manse. As soon as they purchased the classic Georgian Colonial (a meticulously accurate rendering by architect William T. Baker), they knew right away that the décor needed tweaking. The sellers had chosen a spare, Early American palette for much of the house, leaving many rooms feeling cold and gloomy. But the buyers, an active family with young children, longed for warm, vibrant spaces that harmonized with their casual lifestyle.

Eager to feel more at ease in their new home, they tapped Suzanne Kasler to create an updated look. The Atlanta-based decorator, who was named the 2004 Southeast Designer of the Year, gladly tackled the challenge. Taking cues from one of the family's heirloom rugs, Kasler had the living room walls painted in a soft buff tone, and then used the same shade to de-emphasize the ornate details on the ceiling and trim. She added a second layer of color in the fabrics and accessories, pulling in hints of cream, cocoa, sky blue, and rose. And to further ground the space, she introduced a few surprises.

Kasler is known for fusing modern and ethnic elements with purely traditional pieces, crafting a style that's both lighthearted and engaging. For this project she paired a clean-lined Saladino sofa with lavish Fortuny pillows and a gilt-framed antique painting, offering much to talk about in a peaceful conversation nook. In the formal dining room, she took another well-calculated risk by dressing stately Chippendale chairs in whimsical linen "jackets," allowing just enough carved detail to peek through the seams. Uniquely tailored and exquisitely monogrammed, the slipcovers lend a genial look to an otherwise sophisticated room.

Clean, modern lines meet graceful curves in this quiet corner of the living room. The painting, upholstered chair, and elaborate chinoiserie screen are all treasures from the homeowner's personal collection.

Nearby, in the family's casual eating area, Kasler carried the mellow mood one step further. After waxing the walls in a sun-baked shade of taupe, she continued the palette on the trim and fabrics, choosing a muted linen for the chairs and draperies. A cream-colored sisal rug helps to visually lighten the space and further underplay the home's lofty architecture, while a dainty crystal chandelier adds a bit of glamour. "The owners are nice, casual people who love to entertain and spend time with their family," Kasler says. "So my goal was to take this big beautiful house and really make it fit their lifestyle."

Who knew muted gray-green could be so lovely? The earthy shade coats this dining room's molding and wainscoting, providing an artful framework for the hand-painted wallpaper's vivid pastoral scenes.

With a simple vintage farm table at its heart and a whimsical wood-beaded chandelier hanging overhead, this laid back breakfast room evokes the easy elegance and organic beauty of the French countryside.

> "A good Southern house grows and becomes more beautiful with age."

Brown Sugar

As a veteran architect and interior designer, Phillip Sides knows how to listen to houses. One step inside and already he's brimming with ideas and noting the slightest of details. "A house immediately tells you where it needs to go," claims this consummate Montgomery gentleman. "Just pay attention and it'll always send you down the right path."

Following his own advice, Sides took plenty of cues from the enormous scale and classical architecture of the Alabama Symphony Showhouse. Asked to decorate the massively long and tall living room, he knew right away that the space was too big for its own good. "I just couldn't imagine people sitting in there and having a conversation," he says. "It almost felt like a public building."

To create a more intimate feeling in the room, Sides first painted the walls a deep chocolate brown and then laid a huge (and affordable) sisal rug across the entire floor. He chose comfortable, casual furniture—most of it in a rich cream color—that was purposely moderate in scale. And for a final touch, he removed the home's original crystal chandeliers and replaced them with more approachable Japanese paper lanterns.

"The ladies who ran the showhouse almost died when I did that," Sides says with a laugh. "But a showhouse is meant to stimulate you and make you think. Nothing bores me more than doing the same thing over and over again."

RIGHT: A dozen vintage prints, each identically matted and framed, form the focal point in this extra-large living area. Evenly spaced and hung almost to the ceiling, they complement the grand scale of the room and yet help to shrink it down.

OPPOSITE: Against a backdrop of lush, sky blue draperies, this gracefully aged pedestal table holds a wealth of perfectly Southern treasures—including an antique metal lamp, a handsome horse, and an urn awash in magnolias.

Echoing the shape of an armillary sphere from Jim Lanham's collection, the round dining room table is ringed by Anglo-Indian chairs and sensual, lichen-toned walls covered in Travers linen-velvet.

A radiant eighteenth-century Dutch dresser takes center stage in the master bedroom, crowned by two trios of creamware platters and a nineteenth-century German mirror. The gently curving chest is flanked by a pair of antique banister-back chairs.

> "Southern homes used to be very formal. Today, I think most people still want elegance and beauty, but they also demand a good deal of function. Hardly anyone decorates just for looks anymore."

MICHAEL STEINER AND TIM SCHELFE

Family Affair

Michael Steiner and Tim Schelfe are well-versed when it comes to facing design challenges, but this project really had them under the gun. Hired to decorate a custom home near Raleigh, North Carolina, they were given just three months to transform 5,000 square feet (465 sq. m) of living space into a cozy, comfortable retreat. The house needed a subtle overhaul from top to bottom, with plenty of attention to family-friendly details, while also retaining its traditional flavor.

Steiner and Schelfe, who once confronted a similar task with the *Southern Living* Idea Home, decided to focus on texture. Wanting to create a sense of warmth, they were drawn to plush, feel-good fabrics for the soft furnishings and strong, handsome materials like wood and iron for the tables. Because the home had significant architectural detail—including a molded ceiling in the living room and a herringbone floor in the dining room—the designers opted to keep the wall colors fresh and neutral.

"Easy but elegant" became their motto, and the combination proved quite successful. "When we first started, the family room was supposed to be on the second floor," Steiner says. "But the first floor area turned out to be so snug and welcoming that the homeowners now spend most of their time there."

Just because a room is kid-safe doesn't mean it has to be frumpy. The Baker chairs and sofa in this living room all have graceful curves and a dapper appearance. The nearby fire screen is a custom iron piece designed by Michael Steiner.

OPPOSITE: A romantic haven for busy parents, this radiant dining room features a crystal chandelier and silken portieres. The chairs, which are actually quite contemporary, were slipcovered in paisley fabric and trimmed down the back with dressmaker details.

"In my mind, Southern style is about combining antiques that you bought or inherited with looks from the twentieth century. It's that mixture that gives us a true sense of our history."

Shades of Gray

People here still remember what their mama taught them." That's how Jim Smith explains the famously gracious etiquette of Southerners. And he should know. His Baton Rouge firm, Dixon Smith Interiors, was founded by his mother, Dixon Smith, whose classic style and down-to-earth philosophy still guide the business today. She and Jim, along with two other designers, work collaboratively on almost every project, often beginning with a brainstorming session to kick up new ideas.

That's the process they used for this room—a cozy little nook in the Hospice Foundation's Decorator Show House—and their approach worked flawlessly. With no real client to serve, the team created an imaginary homeowner who was "young, cosmopolitan, and liked to travel," and then built the design around this person's mythical lifestyle. Though the room measured just 12'x14' (3.7m × 4.3m), Smith and his crew took a gamble with the wall color, choosing a rich pewter tone that made it feel even more intimate.

They also stretched expectations with their selection of furnishings, opting for a blithe combination of bamboo, sisal, linen, leather, and even a few contemporary accents, despite the very traditional Georgian style of the house. "We weren't trying to be shocking, but we did want to step away from the givens of the architecture," Jim Smith says. "We used one or two antique pieces to set the tone, but then shook it up with things you might not anticipate."

An alluring French tapestry crowns the room like a brilliant jewel, capturing all gazes with its intriguing beauty. By contrast, the nearby Ralph Lauren sofa is a neutral piece that blends quietly into the layout.

OPPOSITE: A perfect example of Dixon Smith mixology, this quaint vignette features an antique dresser, a clean-lined lamp, and a stunning leaf print from the Longstreet Collection. The image is actually a "radiographic photo"—also known as an x-ray.

"My favorite Southern rooms are a little bit fun, a little dressed down, and filled with beautiful natural light."

SUZANNE KASLER

Blended to
Perfection

With its sumptuous textiles and quietly elegant color palette, this gracious Atlanta home is not your typical bachelor pad. A classic red brick Georgian centered on a sweeping double staircase, it exudes a sense of romance and Old World charm, yet it's handsome enough for a fine Southern gentleman. Suzanne Kasler headed up the project, working closely with architects from Kenward Architectural Studio.

The Buckhead-based designer, who envisioned a timeless, welcoming décor, aimed to balance the home's striking traditional features with a liberal dose of comfort and a gentle nod to luxury and beauty. Because the homeowner came to her with virtually no furniture, and was eager to start from scratch, Kasler had the unique opportunity to build her design from the ground up.

"I love rooms that look collected and have a really lovely, distinct patina," she says. "So for this project I gathered pieces that I thought would grow more beautiful over time." In the living room, where soaring ceilings could easily be overpowering, Kasler created warmth by hanging a richly aged antique tapestry. And in the bedroom, where clean and simple is the rule, she added layers of interest by combining myriad textures both new and old.

"If a room has all antiques or all French furniture or all whatever, then nothing stands out," she notes. "But if you have a mix of styles and flavors—and one object that makes a bold statement—that's when a room really comes together."

OPPOSITE: Plush velvet pairs with liquid smooth silk in the formal living room, spawning a look that's both cozy and pleasantly buttoned up. Both upholstered pieces are new, while the tapestry is a wonderfully timeworn, eighteenth-century treasure.

RIGHT: A regal Rose Tarlow bed is the centerpiece of this tranquil master bedroom. Its strong, masculine lines and rich black finish strike a powerful contrast with the room's muted blue-gray walls and whisper-soft silk draperies.

ABOVE: Bathed in natural sunlight and filled with eye-catching textiles, the formal living room exudes feminine charm. The bold tones on the cushions and sofa are a nod to the homeowner's love of luscious color.

OPPOSITE: With a dreamy shade of seafoam on the walls and gauzy linen curtains draped from the canopy bed, this romantic master bedroom is a restful haven that's rich with detail.

"When you can let the outdoors peek in and keep a room crisp and clean, that's Southern style at its best."

Holiday Getaway

Florida's Treasure Coast, which covers a lush expanse along the Southern Atlantic, was originally named for the treasure-filled Spanish galleons that sank off its shores. But today, the most brilliant find in this upscale resort region is not what lies below the waves. It's the tranquil villages that rise above.

Vero Beach, one of the oldest and most beautiful coastal towns, is where you'll find this timeless Southern home. Built as a casual vacation retreat for an Atlanta family, the house has a breezy, mellow feel that perfectly complements the mood of the golf community in which it's located. Dark wood furniture mingles gracefully with lush, jewel-toned fabrics and classical architecture, creating a space that's both refined and cozy.

Designer Rod Mickley, who was tapped to decorate the interior, calls the look "traditional with a tropical twist." Working closely with the homeowners, he artfully melded the clean lines and pared-down beauty of British Colonial style with a light-hearted infusion of vibrant color. "I was trying to bring a sense of freshness to the typical English aesthetic," he says.

Guided by the philosophy that clutter has no place in a vacation atmosphere, Mickley kept every room airy and unfussy by choosing simple furnishings and allowing myriad textures to create depth and interest. In the living room, where dark mahogany tones anchor the space, zebra-print strikes a playful contrast with candy-colored silk. And in the family room, where warm, casual fabrics invite guests to lounge, the walls were left largely unadorned to draw more attention to the view outside.

Another consideration for Mickley was the wealth of architectural detail throughout the house. Nearly every room has intricate moldings and exquisite beamed ceilings, this despite the rooms' relatively small size. To deal with this challenge, he chose light, bright, neutral colors for most of the walls and

opted for simple, natural flooring. Antique chestnut floors span much of the public portion of the home, while hand-woven rugs, most in pale hues, add extra comfort to the bedrooms and other private areas.

"It can be difficult to create warmth and texture and still keep things simple," Mickley says. "But I think most people really feel better in rooms that are balanced—not empty and cold but not busy either." So does this house pass the test? Mickley thinks so. "It's lovely, it's comfortable, and there's not much to dust." What more do you need?

OPPOSITE: This antique Bessarabia rug inspired the rich red palette in the family room. Similar crimson tones are echoed in the cushions of the sea grass club chairs and in the subtle paisley print on the pillows.

BELOW: "Anyone can hang a painting above a bed," says designer Rod Mickley of this delightful mirror collage. To emphasize the lively fabric in this tropical guestroom, he kept most of the accessories simple and sweet.

With few walls and a wide-open layout, this family room didn't
have many options for TV placement. Gretchen Edwards solved
the problem by tucking the TV under the nearby stairs, while
still maintaining an intimate conversation area.

GRETCHEN EDWARDS

Natural
Beauty

No matter how hot and humid it may be outside, this Atlanta home always feels as crisp and fresh as a spring breeze. Designer Gretchen Edwards made sure of that. Building the décor around interesting, natural textures and casual furnishings, she infused the space with a lighthearted, earthy quality that's ideal for a young family on the go.

Initially inspired by the large, exotic painting over the mantel, Edwards devised a vibrant palette of red, cream, chocolate brown, and robin's egg blue. She left the walls a neutral parchment tone—"for a carefree, open look," she says—but then introduced bold color and subtle patterns throughout. The sofas, each upholstered in two different fabrics, endow the room with drama, while the draperies, dotted with tiny eggs and feathers, counterbalance with a bit of whimsy.

For the smaller pieces and accessories, Edwards chose several rustic items from the PierceMartin showroom. In fact, that's how she landed this assignment. Like so many retail shoppers before her, the homeowner had entered the wholesale-only store hoping to make a purchase. But instead of turning her away, the showroom staff recommended Edwards, leading to a collaboration that the designer feels was meant to be. "Right from the start, we were on the same page," she says. "The client was fun and open-minded, and an artist herself, and I think that's why the project came out so well."

Graceful hands and a blue pottery lamp crown what's affectionately known as the "fish table." A striped chenille ottoman and red glazed planter linger not far away.

> "When I think of the South, I think of porches.
> Every good Southern home should have a porch."

MIKE RUEGAMER

Island
Paradise

Off the coast of South Carolina, where white sand beaches weave through meandering blue lagoons, the island community of Hilton Head offers a gracious and leisurely lifestyle. It's here, where stunning natural beauty envelops first-class resort "plantations," that the owners of this mellow beach house decided to build their dream home. Working with architect and designer Mike Ruegamer, they wanted a casual, family-friendly house that maximized the ocean views and gently invited the outdoors in.

It wasn't a new challenge for Ruegamer, whose award-winning firm, Group 3, is based on the island, but the project did pose a unique set of obstacles. The lot was very narrow, with neighboring houses nudging closely on either side. The design had to meet strict standards laid out by the local architectural review board. And then there was the pool—the lone reminder of the home that once stood on this site, and a large, unmovable object around which the entire plan would have to be created.

Faced with substantial exterior hurdles, Ruegamer began by envisioning the details of the interior. He spent time with the owners, took notes on how they used certain rooms, and then tried to craft the ideal indoor environment for their lives. "I'm always thinking in terms of space planning, and my dad was a space planner," he says, "so I like to approach a design in terms of living spaces and really explore how a family might *feel* inside their home."

On this project, he was able to address both form and function by carving out numerous vistas while still affording plenty of privacy. In the kitchen, where a wall of windows flows gracefully into the side yard, the simple interior space is enlivened and sheltered by the gardens outside. At the end of the entry hall, which rises three steps above the living room, a similar visual delight entices the eye, expanding the sense of space and warmly drawing visitors into the heart of the house.

It's an aesthetic that Ruegamer calls "Sea Pines meets the West Indies." Sea Pines, of course, is the development in which the home is located, and it's renowned for its understated architecture and careful preservation of the natural surroundings. Paired with the breezy, quietly elegant style of the West Indies—a lush tropical haven still ripe with Colonial influence—the result is a timeless, seaside retreat that reflects the very best of both worlds.

ABOVE RIGHT: Easy and casual is the key in this laid-back family room, where most of the furniture is slipcovered. The homeowner changes out the green and white covers in the wintertime, replacing them with heavier fabrics in warm beige and chocolate.

OPPOSITE: Made from a combination of pine and mahogany, all of the home's ceiling beams and wide-plank floors were stained a deep dark brown to contrast the neutral walls. Even darker are these Asian cabinets found in an Atlanta antique store.

ABOVE: To streamline the look of the kitchen and draw attention to the unique wall of windows, designer Mike Ruegamer decided to hide most of the appliances. Several are concealed behind this massive granite island.

OPPOSITE: The walls of this light-filled family room are covered in "tabby," the traditional oyster shell stucco that was once used throughout Southern coastal areas. Made entirely from indigenous materials, it also contains lime, sand, and water.

> "My philosophy is that Southern design—or any good design, for that matter—is all about taking something predictable and turning it on its head."

BETH SCHERR

Silver and
Gold

Soft, smooth, earthy beige is the color of choice in this cozy Virginia house—but don't dare call it "neutral." Designer Beth Scherr worked wonders with the limited palette, gently weaving threads of cream, brown, and silver into the mix for a subtle but incredibly luminous effect. Hired by the homeowners after another designer missed the mark, she rose to the challenge by focusing her efforts on texture and detail.

Because the house was architecturally strong, with beautiful nineteenth-century moldings and soaring ceilings, Scherr took cues from its neo-classical style but ultimately bucked the notion of a "period home." Instead, she embraced the traditional feel of the space but gave it her own lighthearted twist. In the dining room, where silver moiré wallpaper sets the mood, she took the metallic theme and ran with it, applying silver leaf to a set of wooden chairs. And in the sitting room, where a warm array of silks and chenilles makes the area feel like a blissful cocoon, Scherr covered a pair of timeless Bergère chairs in an unexpected leopard print.

"I wanted every piece to have some little surprise or interesting quirk," she says, "like an unusual fabric or a fun paint finish. If you look, you'll see elements that are a little bit modern or a bit funky, but overall the house is still very sophisticated. It's traditional, but I think it's ultimately easy to live with."

The leaded glass doors leading to the sitting room originally marked the entrance of an old storefront in Roanoke, Virginia. To complement their exquisite detailing, Beth Scherr painted a similar pattern (in metallic copper) along the top of the drapes.

OPPOSITE: Too much wood! That was the verdict in the dining room, where an existing wooden table was replaced by this twisting tortoiseshell piece from Maitland-Smith. The base of the new table is modeled after an antique; the glass top is purely contemporary.

ABOVE: To accentuate the height of the ceiling and feign the impression of spaciousness, the drapery rod in this easy-going living room is positioned about a foot above the windows.

OPPOSITE: Barely six feet (1.8 m) wide, this tiny kitchen became more functional with the addition of stackable stools and a narrow, rolling table. The worn wood on the hanging cabinet makes the chrome on the stools seem that much sleeker.

PHILLIP SIDES

Gulf Coast
Charm

Good things do come in small packages, as this quaint Florida cottage proves so beautifully. Nestled elbow to elbow between other seaside bungalows in Rosemary Beach, this 1,200-square-foot (111.5 sq. m) gem demanded precise planning and plenty of creative ideas to maximize its limited space. The homeowners wanted seating for eight in their pint-size living room, as well as style and flexibility throughout the house, so they enlisted the help of a trusted friend, Phillip Sides.

The Alabama designer had worked with them on a previous home, and was able to draft a layout for their new living area in ten minutes flat. "Some houses need loud, voluptuous interiors because they have no architecture," Sides says. "And then others just need 'interior eyeshadow' because the architecture is so fabulous." This house, with its elegant French doors, unique woodwork, and open, organic feel, easily fit the latter.

To make the rooms seem bigger and still emphasize their architectural assets, he decided to scale down the size of the furniture and only choose solid pieces that were open at the bottom. Sounds easy enough, but in the end, it took some fancy footwork. With years in the design business—and three *Southern Accents* Idea Homes under his belt—Sides knew it would be difficult to find small-scale furniture that fit the bill. "A lot of what's out there today is very big and poufy," he recalls, "so I went ahead and designed everything myself."

The living room's petite club chairs, which he covered in the same pale blue denim as the sofa, were built to swivel toward one of two conversation areas. And the entertainment center, which artfully conceals a TV and other equipment, was designed to look like a box on stilts. Because it has open shelving at the base, it fools the eye and expands the room's overall sense of space. "Nearly everywhere you look, you see the

floor," Sides says. "And that's what makes the house feel larger."

Another size-enhancing trick: symmetry. Though Sides insists that many of his designs are not perfectly balanced—and that he thrives on every project being fresh and different—he felt strongly that "something about this house just screamed symmetry." By balancing windows, doors, furniture, and even living spaces, he was able to create a mellow, lighthearted look that has, at its heart, a very formal and ordered structure. "It may look effortless," Sides says, "but an awful lot of thought went into it."

ABOVE: Fortune smiled on Phillip Sides the day he found this folded-screen headboard. The perfect size for this wee bedroom, it allowed him to create a sliver of extra space behind the bed.

OPPOSITE: Who can resist a hammock by the sea? Cooled by gentle ocean breezes and blooming with lively island style, this classic Southern porch is an afternoon delight.

Underneath a layer of black marble, Sonia Baltodano discovered original dining room floors made from now-extinct Dade County Pine. Many of the boards were damaged, so she replaced them with salvaged pine and hired a Peruvian craftsman to finish the surface in rubbed wax.

"After Thomas Jefferson discovered Palladian style in Europe, he interpreted it in Monticello, and that was really the birth of classic Southern architecture. The scale is grand, but I think people connect to it on an intuitive level."

SONIA CRUZ DE BALTODANO

Seaside
Revival

Every old house has its secrets, as Sonia Cruz de Baltodano knows all too well. A talented architect with offices on two continents, she spearheaded the renovation of this historic Miami mansion and found plenty of surprises both inside and out. Over the years, the home had veered dramatically from its original Palladian architecture, becoming, as Baltodano says, "undisciplined and dolled up." The exterior had been covered in Victorian detailing, the interior had been muddled by updates, and many of the structural beams had been foolishly severed.

Working with her partner, architect Maria Blanco, Baltodano crafted a very specific blueprint of the changes that needed to be made. Wanting every inch of the house to "speak the same language" and offer maximum functionality, she decided to gut the entire structure and add on two new sprawling wings. "Palladian architecture is based on the designs of European farms and manor houses," she says, "so it's very comfortable and masculine, with a seamless flow to the outdoors. That's what we needed to restore in this home."

Her new design called for generous, light-filled rooms, spilling open to lush courtyards and loggias, with a definite emphasis on entertaining. All of the furniture was chosen (as you might expect from a cozy beach house) with an eye toward lounging and leisure. "This is definitely not a pretentious place," Baltodano says of the reworked abode. "It's happy and lovely now—just as it was always meant to be."

Echoing the roots of the home's architecture, an Italian artisan coated all of the walls in Venetian putty. Soft, simple furnishings were chosen to complement this rustic look, with cheerful slipcovered pieces and English antiques dominating the living room.

Loads of natural light spills into the main living room at the Hope & Glory, where a folk art cabinet by local craftsman **Brad Stephens** matches the playful spirit of the bold checkered floor. Before renovation, the large open space comprised four separate rooms.

> "Having grown up in the North and Midwest, I think the South has such a wonderfully casual, carefree sense about it. Life here is always just a little more relaxed."

"Inn" the
Mood

It's not often that you get to help someone follow a dream and then have your own dream come true in the process, but that's exactly what happened to Lisa Sherry. Several years ago, when her friend Bill Westbrook decided to leave his job, move across country, and renovate an old schoolhouse, he asked her if she'd lend a hand. He was opening an inn, he told her, creating a masterpiece from a rundown wreck, and what he needed was a good designer.

It was an enticing proposal for Sherry, who lived in Minneapolis at the time, but there was one small hitch. The project was 1,300 miles (2,100 km) away in Virginia, and she was not, nor had she ever been, an interior designer. Her background was in photo styling, arranging staged scenes for advertising campaigns, but that was just fine with Westbrook. For the inn—which was later christened the Hope & Glory—he envisioned a snapshot-perfect image around every corner.

"Right away, I knew this wasn't your typical bed and breakfast," Sherry says. "Bill had such an amazing vision, even when the rest of us thought he was nuts." What he didn't have was a huge budget. To afford the extensive renovations *and* be able to decorate the building, he challenged Sherry to create a shoestring design scheme.

Westbrook wanted a warm, whimsical environment, a carefree place bubbling with charm, but he didn't give much direction beyond that. So with minimal funds and a lot of leeway, Sherry did what any clever shopper would do. She headed to the nearest flea market. Buying scores of well-worn furnishings and odd bits of architectural salvage, she eventually filled a 24-foot (7.3 m) moving van with her treasures, and drove them all the way from Minnesota to Virginia.

A neutral palette doesn't detract from the lighthearted tone of this casual cottage. Lisa Sherry added bold color with her accessories, and a dash of natural texture with a found birch sapling.

After painting each of the rooms in a fresh earth tone, Sherry hired a seamstress to whip up inexpensive curtains on the spot, using leftover fabric or lengths of sheer cotton. For headboards, she pieced together salvaged columns and old picket fence boards, and for accessories she used an array of found objects and folk art pieces from local craftspeople. "So many quirky things came out of the fact that we didn't have a lot of money," Sherry says proudly. "I think it really forced me to be creative, but it was also a heck of a lot of fun."

Crisp robin's egg blue coats the walls in this soothing bathroom retreat. Antique mirrors, a gauzy mosquito net, and a simple iron egg basket—all painted bright white—provide interest without adding clutter.

In deciding that this room would have a more masculine feel, Lisa Sherry painted the walls in a restful beige and opted for simple linens and black accessories. The straw hat lampshade is an old favorite.

ABOVE: A lovely flurry of secondhand finds complements the easy, breezy style of this ranch house loggia. Its mostly muted palette is animated by saucy bursts of bold color.

OPPOSITE: "This is a vacation home, so I tried not to take anything too seriously," says Jon Vaccari, referring to the clearly tongue-in-cheek décor of this quaint cottage bedroom. "It's a small space with odd angles, so I just ran with it."

Rustic design speaks softly of days gone by, weaving a sylvan tale of honest materials and age-old techniques. Its warm-hearted rooms are always ripe with nature's graces.

Rustic

OPPOSITE: Lustrous wood tones yield to the simple shape of a handmade chair in this sublimely elegant rustic entry hall.

ABOVE: Bathed in sunlight and full of honest, natural textures, the living room has a restful, easygoing air about it. The wide-plank wooden floors, which anchor the space, were crafted from a variety of un-planed timbers.

OPPOSITE: Salvaged from another building, the old long-leaf pine used for the kitchen cabinets was initially covered in peeling paint. Gloria Frame found the surface too distracting so she blowtorched and waxed it until it was smooth and uniform.

> "A Southern home should be a haven. It can be graceful and sophisticated, but more than anything it should be comfortable."

Cabin Fever

Like many strong Southern women before her, Gloria Frame isn't afraid to bend the rules. Eager to chase her own muse and tackle life like a great adventure, she decided to build an unconventional lake house using all salvaged materials, and not a single soul could convince her otherwise. After purchasing three historic log cabins sight unseen, Frame had them shipped from North Carolina to Texas, where she planned to combine them into one unified structure.

On her lush five-acre plot at the edge of Lake Travis, she imagined a cozy, rustic house that rambled gracefully across the landscape and looked as if it had been there forever. Contractors doubted he;, builders scoffed and fled; but Frame pressed on until finally she found a willing accomplice. That turned out to be a scrappy old-timer—a vagabond former literature professor who, amazingly, specialized in log cabin construction—and for six months solid, he lived and worked out of a camp tent on Frame's property.

"The man hadn't cut his hair in probably twenty years," she says with a hoot. "He'd sit out there and cook beans on his little stove, and sometimes he'd go jump in the lake or squirt himself with the hose!"

He also fought tooth and nail with Frame anytime she challenged his expertise. "If I told him that a wall wasn't straight or that something wasn't square, he'd say, 'Lady, it's a log cabin. It's not supposed to be square!'" After one particularly volatile argument, the builder walked off the job, with Frame quite happy to see him go. Thankfully, most of the major construction was completed at that point, and she was left to focus on the interiors.

Wanting a clean, sophisticated look that was also comfortable, she elected to keep the furnishings minimal and allow the exposed

timbers to be the focal point. "A good house stands on its own," Frame says. "You shouldn't need a lot of frills." To create multiple layers of texture, she incorporated wicker, iron, stone, and richly hued plaster. She also selected a handful of plush fabrics to soften the rooms and add color, all of which were decidedly unfussy.

Like her mentor and former boss, famed designer John Saladino, Frame prefers a down-to-earth aesthetic that allows architecture to speak louder than accessories. "John used to joke that he'd like to develop a 'chintz repellant,'" she says, laughing. "That is definitely something I'd use!"

Textured plaster and tumbled marble give the bathroom a sense of age. Throughout the house, a crew of Hispanic craftsmen especially skilled in the art of Old World plastering worked on both the walls and the chinking in between the timbers.

Old beams and leftover rafters form the basic structure of the carriage house, which Gloria Frame now uses as her office. The small living area features a cozy loft area and a wall of barn-style doors.

ABOVE: Fortuny fabric graces a Louis XVI chair in the dining room. The nearby piano, which once filled with water during a thunderstorm, is now used as a display table instead of an instrument.

OPPOSITE: Never afraid to mix genres, Gwynn Griffith pairs three early American "naïve" portraits with a modern 1960s hand chair in her foyer. She bought the chair directly from artist Pedro Friedeberg and credits it with inspiring her career.

> "Southern style runs from one gamut to another. It covers the waterfront. But when it has a little Mexican or Spanish influence, that's always wonderful."

Lone Star
Lovely

Take a drive through southern San Antonio and you're bound to notice it—a soaring old brick building that seems to rise out of nowhere. Surrounded by Victorian bungalows and idyllic tree-lined streets, this former factory stands in striking contrast to the "normal" homes nearby. And that suits owner Gwynn Griffith just fine. The feisty Texas designer, who counts some of Hollywood's finest among her clientele, is never one to follow the crowd.

She bought this massive structure ten years ago, when it was nothing more than an empty shell, and slowly, with lots of elbow grease and an ever-evolving sense of style, she has transformed it into a warm, welcoming, and eclectic loft. "I don't like predictable," she says, "so I guess that's why this place appealed to me." Though the three-story factory once housed a shoe manufacturer, a metal fabricator, a seed company, and even a tortilla-whirling communist, by the time Griffith moved in, it had been abandoned for decades and was left with no interior walls, no defined rooms, and no updated systems.

As soon as Griffith saw the building's huge windows and high ceilings, she instantly knew that it was the "house" for her. Adopting a learn-on-the-fly approach to remodeling, she began the project by erecting a few walls, tearing a few down, and then erecting a few more, all in search of the perfect layout. Finally satisfied (and with new plumbing and electric installed at last), Griffith asked her son, painter Greg Mannino, to distress the walls and "knock them back to another century." The entire loft, she had decided, would evoke the feeling of "Spanish mission meets Italian villa"—gracious, aged, and pleasantly imperfect.

To realize her vision, Griffith scoured local salvage yards for recycled doors and columns that would match the scale of the

building. She then filled the space—all 11,000 square feet (1,022 sq. m) of it—with an intriguing, always changing hodgepodge of her favorite things. Oil paintings, lush textiles, religious artifacts, and antique furniture. All bring a sense of warmth and coziness to this Texas-size home, a unique place that, Griffith admits, is something of a local curiosity. "It may seem unorthodox from the outside, but it's really very orthodox once you're inside," she says.

And what about the rumor that the loft is haunted? "Nah, it's not haunted," Griffith says with a laugh. "But if you don't close the windows during a storm, the rugs will rise right up off the floor."

Opposites attract in the light-filled kitchen, where a heavily
carved Mexican table shares the stage with a streamlined sink.
Both the sink and the countertop were crafted from salvaged
marble found at an old soda fountain.

Influenced by Mexican style, the bathroom features a simple pine cabinet, a pair of sconces, and a portrait of San Antonio's namesake, St. Anthony. The mural is based on the work of Renaissance painter Piero Dell a Francesca.

The front façade of this handsome bar was once a hefty old door used during the World's Fair in New Orleans. The painting—an 1850s portrait of a musical matriarch—was found in a far-flung Mexican village.

> "Southern homes always have a classic sense of proportion. They also have warm, comfortable rooms that help an owner to extend hospitality."

Collective Soul

Growing up, Peggy Westerman dreamed of being an archeologist, and today that rogue spirit still serves her well. A designer, developer, and all-around Renaissance woman, she savors the chance to blaze a new trail or roll up her sleeves, especially when it comes to her house. A sprawling Baton Rouge abode designed by family friend and famous Southern architect A. Hays Town, Westerman's home is a true labor of love.

"I've sanded every single beam in here," she says proudly, referring to the massive salvaged timbers that she personally rescued and recycled. A keen stickler for authentic details, Westerman has installed heart pine floors and antique cypress doors (or what she calls "good, honest, old wood") in nearly every room, believing that it adds incomparable warmth and substance. She has also used a wealth of antique hardware and traditional light fixtures throughout the house, adding yet another layer of authenticity to her wonderfully rustic décor.

Befitting the style of the architecture—New Orleans Courtyard with 1790s detailing and an artful mélange of French, Spanish, and Mexican influences—Westerman has filled her home with many hard-won historical treasures. Traveling far and wide to unearth rare paintings and brilliant tapestries, this passionate collector has walked out of remote villages carrying artifacts and artwork on her back. And she values the adventure almost as much as the find.

"My house and everything in it has been one big journey," Westerman says, quite satisfied. "Every time I come home, it's like arriving back with a good friend."

"Certain pieces just communicate to me," Peggy Westerman says of her seventeenth-century religious artwork. Many of the items in her collection, including this exquisite Mexican colonial painting of St. Dominic, "have a sweet simplicity that's just amazing."

> "I think you define Southern style by blending old and new in a comfortable, elegant way, and going with your own personal gut instinct. It's that simple."

BABS WATKINS

Saving
Grace

On a high hill in Texas, where a canopy of stars embraces the landscape, is where you'll find this rustic masterpiece. Created as a cozy weekend escape for a Houston family, it's both daringly modern and faithfully traditional, with the roots of its design planted firmly in the past. At the center of the structure, literally, is an old cottage built by German immigrants in the nineteenth century. Handcrafted from indigenous pink stone, it inspired the style and scale of the adjoining "barn" and "sister houses"—the three thoughtful additions envisioned by architect Don B. McDonald and decorator Babs Watkins.

Comfort was a top priority for the homeowners, who wanted a casual gathering place for entertaining. Also concerned with preservation, they insisted on maintaining the historical integrity of the original cottage, while seamlessly integrating the new construction. For McDonald, that meant finding traditional craftsmen and authentically old materials. For Watkins, it signaled an eighteen-month odyssey of collecting furniture and accessories. "The goal was to make it look as if the house had been there forever," Watkins says. "Everything we used needed to complement the unique heritage of the property, from the kitchen cabinets to the doors and the floors."

As a veteran shop owner specializing in European antiques, she knew exactly where to look. Focusing her efforts in France and

ABOVE RIGHT: Reminders of the original 1830s cottage can still be seen in this restful living room, where an eclectic mix of French and Italian furniture is accented by artwork. The niche is an antique from Italy, while the painting comes from the homeowners' own studio.

OPPOSITE: Towering beams, all salvaged from old buildings, offer a striking focal point in this grand but comfy media room. As the main living area in the house, the space flows easily into the kitchen, the screened porch, and the foyer.

Italy, Watkins honed in on bucolic pieces with a hint of sophistication, often choosing gracefully timeworn items that had been built or painted by hand. "The family was absolutely amazing during the whole process," she says. "They turned everything over to me and put incredible trust in my judgment. That really added to the uniqueness of this project."

When Watkins wasn't searching for furnishings, she joined ranks alongside McDonald and a crew of unusually talented craftsmen, in an environment she calls "wonderfully electric." Master artisan Jay Iarussi, who spent weeks aging the walls with paint and plaster, often flooded the home with the sounds of classical music. And the German stone masons, who offered rare insight on old-fashioned building techniques, always enlivened the already colorful atmosphere.

"I can't tell you how much fun I had working on this house," Watkins beams. "All of us recognized the importance of details on this job, no matter how small. And everyone—the architect, the assistants, even the moving guy—was encouraged to contribute to the design. I'm so proud of this. I really am. And I know the family loves it too."

ABOVE: "Pure bliss" is the only way to describe this wonderfully warm bedroom in one of the "sister houses." Simple and mellow, with casual French furnishings, it's a welcome haven for guests and family members.

OPPOSITE: With the massive barn doors rolled back, you can see straight through the dining room and kitchen, where a sweeping country vista awaits just beyond. "There's really no line here between inside and out," says Babs Watkins.

> "There's a definite style to the South. It's very gracious and understated, and a little bit quirky."

Sticks and
Stones

After two decades in the design business, including several years under the wing of Zelina Brunschwig (of Brunschwig & Fils fame), Candy Lloyd has never met a room she couldn't improve. The daughter of a talented decorator who grew up believing that all mothers were as stylish as hers, the Atlanta-based designer has faced many challenges in her career, but this project really tested her mettle.

A rugged weekend retreat in the South Carolina countryside, the property was built using massive log timbers and hearty boulders. Created in a grand chalet style reminiscent of soaring mountain homes, it was designed to be comfortable and casual, with kick-off-your-shoes ambiance and nary a hint of urban pretense. That was the big picture, but the devil was in the details.

As with many household ventures, the couple who owned the home had very different views about how it should materialize. The wife, thinking of family gatherings and cozy nights by the fire, insisted on lovely, plush fabrics and cushy furniture. The husband, operating from a more masculine mindset, decided that the house needed, well, lots of storage.

A veteran big game hunter, he had amassed a large taxidermy collection that, despite the best objections of his wife, he wanted to prominently display. Designer Lloyd, hoping to please both parties, was asked to craft a double-sided décor that could seam-

lessly meld each of the two visions. On one hand, she would set aside space for the husband's collection, creating durable, hard-working rooms where he could welcome fellow hunters. On the other, she would pepper the home with feminine accents and carefully carve out spaces that were absolutely animal-free.

"It was all a matter of compromise," Lloyd says graciously. "But that's the case in every house. You're always looking for ways to meet the needs of everyone involved." This project just happened to feature a unique scenario, in more ways than one. Not only did Lloyd have to balance the wishes of the homeowners, but she also had to handle the structure itself. Because the walls are made from log beams, she had to find creative ways to use color. And because the scale of each room is so immense, she faced the additional battle of finding the right-size furnishings.

"No doubt about it, this house really pushed me," Lloyd admits.

ABOVE RIGHT: Lavish velvets and chenilles predominate in the family-friendly living room, where oversized furnishings make the space feel smaller and more down-to-earth. The lush fabrics help to balance the texture of the wood plank walls.

OPPOSITE: "Mixing oddball fabrics" is a specialty of Candy Lloyd, who warmed up this sprawling dining room space by pairing yellow patterned linen with rich red paisley. To carry the same tones into the adjoining kitchen, she gently aged the cabinets with a faux finish.

The homeowner had her heart set on a dressing table, but she may not have imagined this—a rough-cut log skirted in plaid silk and topped with two Majolica lamps. This room, by the way, is one of only three in the house with wallpapered walls.

"I didn't want a typical movie-set lodge feel," Candy Lloyd says. For this pretty guest bedroom, the designer chose simple, country-style fabrics and a pair of graceful gourd lamps with hand-painted shades.

"There's a big hand-me-down quality to the South, whether it's furniture or music or folk tales. I think Southerners like to keep tradition going."

Sweet Georgia Brown

Some designers revel in their signature style, forever producing carbon copies of the same rooms, but not Bill Stewart. "I'd much rather develop someone's quirks," says the Atlanta style maestro. Intrigued by the notion of blurring the lines between decades, he likes nothing better than to fuse contemporary furniture and vintage finds with odd artifacts that the client has loved forever.

For this lively Georgia home, which looms in the treetops over Lake Lanier, his inspiration was two-fold: the owners' interesting art collection, and quite surprisingly, the classic lodges of the great national parks. Enamored with the nostalgic appeal of these favorite vacation spots, he incorporated many of their trademark features into his plan—stacked stone, generous rafters, and of course, espresso brown shingles. The exterior is covered in those.

Stewart also borrowed the lodges' laid-back ambiance, adopting a plucky, youthful approach to artwork and accessories. After painting the living room in a lush shade of apple green, he embellished it up with a massive cuckoo clock, a dreamy Lawrence Gipe painting, a timeworn gear table, and a 1950s scale model boat that, he says, "reeks of atmosphere." Elsewhere in the house, he further mingled rustic elements with clean lines, creating hip, comfortable rooms that aren't afraid to be fun.

"The sense of discovery should be just as exciting," Stewart says, "whether you're winding your way through a flea market, or walking down a trail, or looking at the stuff in your own home."

ABOVE: In the TV room, all eyes are drawn to this technicolor tile fireplace, which playfully hobnobs with a palm frond tiki and heavily carved antique mirror. "The art is in the mix," Stewart says of the eccentric grouping.

OPPOSITE: As a nod to the man of the house, who works for Kravet Fabrics, Bill Stewart used one of the company's washed chenilles to cover the living room sofas. He designed the light fixtures.

ABOVE: A tapestry of textures is woven into this vibrant breakfast nook, where an Italian marbled table shines under the soft glow of a Venini chandelier. The chairs were a favorite find of Jon Vaccari, who has since reproduced them for clients.

OPPOSITE: This 1940s-style corner banquette is an exclusive Vaccari design, upholstered in silky Rogers & Goffigon fabric and teamed with a Moroccan rug and table. The painting is by artist Hunt Slonem.

> "Being inside all the time is just not what it's about in the South. People entertain a lot, and they like to get out and enjoy their surroundings."

JON VACCARI

French Quarter
Flair

Buying an old house is always a bit of a gamble, but when it's an 1820s slave quarters with bland 1950s updates, the odds are definitely not good. Unless, of course, you're Jon Vaccari. For this talented New Orleans designer, whose eye for potential is incredibly fine-tuned, a project of such magnitude is not only possible; it's almost guaranteed to succeed.

Several years ago, Vaccari announced that he'd found the perfect fixer-upper—a smallish home with low ceilings and no air conditioning—and everyone thought he was crazy, even his mom. But where friends and family saw a money pit, the designer and his partner, Steve Fleming, saw nothing but "good bones and a great location." Tucked away on a quiet street in the French Quarter, the house oozed with atmosphere, recalling the souls and secrets of nearly 200 years. Unfortunately, it also revealed decades of inattention.

"As soon as we bought it, I wanted it all," Vaccari says, "a pool, a patio, fountains, parking." But the pragmatic approach eventually won him over. Because the original footprint of the house was just 1,700 square feet, (158 sq. m) he and Fleming kicked off eight months of construction with an ambitious 1,100-square-foot (102 sq. m) addition. They also increased ceiling heights in the original structure from eight feet to ten, replaced most of the flooring with red pine, and added a wealth of decorative trim and antique French doors. Still, the place took some getting used to.

"We went from a grand home with fourteen-foot (4.3 m) ceilings to a smaller, more cottage-style home," Vaccari explains. "Our old furniture didn't fit, so we just had to start over." Longing for a charming but fun and funky space, they decided to fuse Hollywood glamour with a twist of Moroccan spice, keeping the

lines clean and the overall feeling quite comfortable. "I wanted the interior to say something about who we are and to reflect our interests and our travels," Vaccari says.

In the kitchen, that wish was translated into a goulash of colors and textures, which included exotic blue-and-yellow tiles, a massive French gothic bookcase, and a show-stealing painting by Juan Loredo. In the master bedroom, where the palette is whisper-soft, the focus hinged more on warm, whimsical accents and the irresistible lure of the gardens below. "I'm never afraid to mix things up," Vaccari says confidently. "I think it's infinitely more interesting when you just quit worrying about 'the rules' and have fun. It's your house, so why not?"

In this fresh all-white sitting area, the fireplace is flanked by iron lemon trees found at a villa in St. Tropez. Beneath the goat hair rug, the floor splits into stripes, alternating between original planks and red pine.

Simple and sweet is the theme of the master bedroom, which offers a safe haven even for Fred the dachshund. Airy curtains by Creation Baumann envelop the French doors, while leafy fabric from Larsen covers the bench and headboard.

Just like the famed late designer Sister Parish, Helaine Moyse likes to blend formal and informal, upscale and bargain-priced. On the bedside table she pairs a "hideously expensive" Plexiglas lamp with pricey cotton and raffia fabric and an inexpensive green basket.

> "Southern style revolves around beautiful heirlooms, lovely fabrics, and trying to create coolness and calmness in our hot and spicy climate."

HELAINE MOYSE

Joie de
Vivre

Happy-go-lucky might be the best way to describe Helaine Moyse's work. Fun and fresh, with not a hint of heaviness, it bubbles over with feel-good charm and a sense of effortless grace—much like Helaine herself. The veteran designer, whose surname ('MO-ease') rings with delightful Southern cadence, approaches every project as if it were a canvas just waiting to be splashed with color.

That's how she tackled the tremendous scope of the *Southern Living* Idea House, and how she envisioned these two lovely rooms as well. Both of the latter spaces were featured in the Hospice Foundation's Decorator Showcase Home, and both reveal Moyse's attention to detail and composition. Rich with texture and brightened by a cool, crisp palette, each offers a sundry mix of styles and accessories.

The sitting room was designed to have a treehouse feel, with light, simple furnishings that complement, rather than compete with the natural surroundings outside. The bedroom was inspired by Tiffany's—or rather the color of the famous jeweler's box. After coating the walls in that exact shade, Moyse added a custom-made iron bed, a lilac blanket from Kmart, several landscape paintings by Louisiana artist Lisa diStefano, and her favorite accents, silver and baskets.

"Every room needs silver and baskets," she says with a laugh. "What good is a house that doesn't have a sense of humor?"

Breezy white curtains set the stage for this mellow sunroom, where vibrant pink pillows (made from French mattress ticking) rub elbows with a custom-made iron daybed. Out front, an old Oriental garden seat rests atop a cowhide.

"Vistas and views. Porches, loggias, terraces. When you get down to it, the main facet of Southern living is the openness to nature and the outdoors."

JOSEPH MINTON

European Ease

Look closely at any room fashioned by Joseph Minton and you're bound to see the flavors of myriad cultures and far-flung locales. This renowned Texas designer, whose work has graced the pages of top magazines for nearly 35 years, is also a consummate globetrotter with an eye for fine foreign treasures. Artfully blending elegant French antiques with rustic pine furniture and even a hint of Asian flair, he favors a hodgepodge approach to decorating, and the result is always wonderful.

For this project—an enchanting family home in Dallas—Minton used his signature formula with typical panache. Challenged to create a warm, aged feeling in a newly constructed space, he glazed the stucco walls in a lush parchment shade and then devised his primary palette from the baked earth tones of an Oriental rug. Bold cinnabar sofas punctuate the living room, while hints of red linger more quietly in the mostly muted dining area.

Overall the mood is Mediterranean, with formal and casual elements striking a comfortable balance. "I like to throw old rustic pieces into a formal room, and maybe a little gilt into a rustic setting," Minton admits. Just as long as it doesn't seem contrived. "I can't think of anything worse than a house that looks like a decorator just walked out," he says. "It's much more interesting when it feels collected and searched for over time."

RIGHT: Exquisite copies abound in the dining room. The table is modeled after a sixteenth-century piece, while the chairs are based on originals from the Vatican. An authentic Julio Larraz painting casts a fanciful backdrop.

OPPOSITE: In layering various textures in the living room, Joseph Minton paired plush fabrics with rusty hammered iron. The coffee table, named "Giaco" after Swiss artist Alberto Giacometti, is a custom piece from his Minton-Corley furniture line.

> "A good Southern home should be interesting, even on the ceiling. Rather than just plain old white, do something—wallpaper, stenciling, grass cloth—to dress it up."

MIMI MCMAKIN AND BROOKE HUTTIG

Palm Beach
Pizzazz

In the halcyon haven of Palm Beach, Florida, the traditional winter home of the world's über affluent, only one name is synonymous with classic Palm Beach style— that's Kemble Interiors. A staple of upper-crust society for nearly two decades, the design firm founded by Mimi McMakin and Brooke Huttig is famous for its joyful colors and casually elegant spaces, all punctuated by a liberal dose of fun. "We like comfortable, easy-to-live-in houses with a touch of whimsy," Huttig says. "Our designs always have a little something out of the ordinary to catch your eye."

For this breezy vacation home in Vero Beach, that "little something" is the array of textures, including the vibrant hibiscus fabric leaping boldly from the living room. "The flowers are huge, and can you believe those giant seedpods?" McMakin asks. Another show-stopper, the daybed-sized coffee table, is rumored to be from a Chinese opium den. And the leopard-print ottoman, which steals glances with its bauble-heavy bullion fringe, adds a bit of sauce to this otherwise serene setting.

"We have plenty of clients who long for the perfect English house or the perfect French house," McMakin says. "But this client just wanted a place where she could relax with her husband and children and have a good time." To capture that bucolic feel, McMakin and Huttig chose a relaxing palette of

blue, white, and yellow, with the master bedroom adorned in shades of sky, soft ivory, and dark-toned wood.

The homeowner couldn't decide on a particular fabric for the space, so McMakin, unfazed, announced, "Great! We'll use them all!" Snowy matelassé was picked for the slipcovered pieces (inspired by similar fabric from a hotel in Capri), while a creamy white coverlet dripping with tassels was ordained as the bedspread. Elsewhere in the house, the designers revved the color up a notch, opting for cheery yellow walls in the living room and kissable pale pink in the bathroom.

Pink, in fact, is one of their signature colors, often paired with perky apple green. "We just love to re-create spring," McMakin says. "There isn't a woman who doesn't look pretty in pink, and that's what Florida is all about." That, apparently, and pigs. In every Kemble-designed home, she and Huttig poke at least one pig into the décor—like the inconspicuous wicker ottoman in this home. "What can I say?" laughs McMakin. "If you've got people sitting on pigs, you know it's going to be a great party."

ABOVE RIGHT: A vivid harmony of fabrics sets the master bedroom aglow. Dressing up the four-poster Mike Bell bed are lush pillows from Raoul Textiles and a trio of botanical prints overhead.

OPPOSITE: Faux *bois* columns support soaring archways in this light-filled living room. "Eclectic" is definitely the word for the various textiles used, with a bold mix of stripes, solids, and patterns artfully intertwined.

OPPOSITE: This simple iron bed is softened with an ethereal linen canopy, tied on with rustic twine and dangling seashells. Guests can enjoy the simplicity of this relatively spare room, focusing on the subtle shapes and textures rather than eye-popping color.

RIGHT: A dazzling, seashell-encrusted chandelier is the obvious focal point in this sublime bathroom. The ocean theme is carried over in the wallpaper and mirror, while the bamboo molding accents take a decidedly tropical turn.

> "We're lucky to live in such a great vacation atmosphere. To really take full advantage of that, I think a Southern home needs to be airy and uncluttered."

Tropical Punch

Like the Canadian family that owns this festive Florida home, Rod Mickley knows the importance of sun and fun. A native Northerner who weathered many winters before finally heading south, this leading Vero Beach-based designer tries to take full advantage of his tropical environs. In every seaside space he creates, Mickley arouses a sense of mellowness and lazy-day leisure by using casual fabrics and comfortable, lounge-around furnishings.

He usually chooses a breezy palette of soft, natural colors, but for this project the clients had very specific hues in mind. They wanted an overall scheme of cool blues and whites throughout most of the house, but in one room—a cozy little nook for reading and relaxing—they had their sights set on bold. Eager to experience a true island atmosphere, they liked the idea of splashy fabrics, bright walls, and just a hint of Caribbean sophistication.

Mickley responded by drawing inspiration from the local community, which features a wealth of British Colonial architecture. Pairing dark-stained wood pieces with vibrant red-and-yellow pillows and West Indies artwork, he was able to strike a perfect balance between upscale and utterly charming. "The colors are quite striking," Mickley says, "but the room is so fun and fresh that the whole family really likes spending time in there."

ABOVE: Anchored by an eye-catching plaid sofa, this tranquil living room embraces a variety of styles. The table is British Colonial, many of the accessories have an ocean theme, and the lamps (an original Rod Mickley design) are based on old candle stands from a church.

OPPOSITE: The variety of textures in this sunny family room strikes a balance between earthy and elegant. Red and yellow fabrics meld with natural woven materials for a look that's easy but upscale.

Amidst a sea of earth tones and natural textures throughout the house, the kitchen's eye-popping crimson cabinets are the ultimate exclamation point. Brilliant and glossy, with slick black granite countertops nearby, they're painted the same color as the home's front door.

> "Designing a house where the inside and outside flow seamlessly—that's the challenge in a beautiful environment like the South."

ERIC WATSON

Better Off
Red

No doubt about it, Eric Watson is a detail man. The Tampa-based architect, who designs custom homes along the Gulf Coast, can somehow weave every nuance of a project into his overall vision. Every color, every curve, every window serves a purpose for him. And on this venture—a cozy vacation villa in Rosemary Beach—it was especially true.

Inspired by a trip to the Caribbean, where many plantation homes still reflect the influence of British Colonialism, Watson approached this design with one primary goal. By melding the careful symmetry of Elizabethan architecture with the breezy openness of a seaside cabana, he aimed to create a modern new house that had, in its details, a gracious old soul.

He built the structure around a central entry area, then devised a "bookended scheme" with bedrooms and other private spaces on either side. He also placed the living room on the second floor for added privacy, leaving the bedrooms downstairs. When it came to the bones of the house—the ceilings, doorways, floors, and structural elements—Watson remained true to history, using what he calls "straightforward, natural materials" in a very traditional way.

"I tried to use classic detailing but update the layout and make it fresh," he says. "Now I think the home feels warm and comfortable, like an old house does, but it's updated for the way people live today." The judges of the prestigious Palladio Award thought so too—they recently honored him for this innovative project.

To contrast the living room's rustic pine ceiling, decorator Susan Massey (who shared design duties with Eric Watson) chose an array of sensual fabrics and muted colors. Bold punches of red and chartreuse add a light-hearted sense of vibrancy to the space.

> "Southerners are very open-hearted people. We live with lots of space around us, so we're more open to our surroundings."

Aging Gracefully

When it comes to decorating,

Phillip Sides is a man of strong convictions. He doesn't do trendy. He abhors clutter. And this lauded Gulf Coast designer, known for his crisp, collected style, admits he's practical to a fault. "If a client wants an all-white room, I'm sorry, I just can't do it," Sides says emphatically. "I see a lot of work in magazines and think, 'Does anybody live there?' I detest spaces that are pure stage sets."

In Sides' own home—a wonderfully robust apartment in Montgomery—the décor falls decidedly within his rules. Warm and welcoming, with a hodgepodge of elegant treasures, it's carefully edited and immensely down-to-earth. The kind of place that sets you longing for a good book, the 1918 dwelling exudes a sense of refinement but without feeling stodgy or bland.

Sides fell in love with it at first sight, ignoring the fact that the apartment had deep fuchsia walls and an array of age-related issues. "The light and the view stopped me in my tracks," he says. "It felt like being in Central Park." Indeed, the view *was* crafted by Frederick Law Olmsted, the famed landscape architect who planned Sides' neighborhood in the 1800s and also designed Central Park. Its clean, ordered layout, countered by a wild expanse of lush greenery, appealed to Sides' own architectural sensibilities and ultimately sealed the deal.

As soon as the designer moved into the apartment, he set out to restore some of the unit's original detailing. He repaired

crumbling woodwork and installed new multi-pane windows, and then turned his sights to decorating. Choosing a palette of warm almond with muted golds and greens, Sides shied away from bold colors to allow textures and shapes to take center stage. Serpentine sconces, clouded mirrors, and lustrous old fabrics all came alive under his tutelage, forming a beautiful montage of vibrant patinas. A self-confessed "junk hound," he mixed old with new, rough with smooth, and drew from a lifetime of shopping flea markets and antique stores to choose the perfect mix of furnishings.

"If I get one more thing I'll have to rake it all out," Sides laughs. Or else just move. Despite the effort poured into this apartment, the Alabama native is now spending most of his time in Florida, where his new store, Phillip & Co, just opened in Rosemary Beach. "I may have a new home," he says, "but my heart is still in the same old place."

ABOVE RIGHT: A consummate fan of Gothic style, Phillip Sides couldn't resist this sinuous chandelier. Underneath is a $220 (£115) table from an auction and a quartet of antique leather chairs.

OPPOSITE: This regal two-headed lamp was once a doorstop. Sides had it converted and then teamed it with a nostalgic blend of old-fashioned finds. The chest below is an original Biedermeier.

ABOVE: An old mahogany bed forms the centerpiece of this incredibly restful bedroom, where two cane-back chairs echo the wood tone of two rustic bamboo window shades. A row of chenille blankets hangs behind the bed.

OPPOSITE: Included in this decadent hallway vignette is a seventeenth-century box, a swath of printed velvet, and a dreamy eighteenth-century mirror that looks almost like a portal to another time. Phillip Sides hung the velvet from a rusted rod, saying, "I prefer an old piece of iron to a fine piece of silver."

OPPOSITE: Turquoise and brown is a favorite color combo of Lee Ledbetter, who used it to conjure a sense of restfulness in his master bedroom. Wanting "soothing but with surprises," he teamed a boldly patterned Stark rug with an Edward Wormley slipper chair and a bed of his own design.

LEFT: Vintage low-profile chairs make for interesting bedfellows with the thirteen-foot ceilings in the living and dining rooms. Though first designed for homes of shorter stature, they work beautifully in this space.

> "In terms of high style, I think there's a deep respect for things that are old and good in the South. There's a great respect here for things that have been passed down."

Debonair Details

Like the dapper Cary Grant character in one of his favorite films—Hitchcock's *North by Northwest*—Lee Ledbetter is a wry, resourceful, sophisticated kind of guy. A bastion of great style in a city of celebrated tastemakers, the New Orleans-based architect is renowned for his sublime interiors and sleek, modern aesthetic. He's infamous for designing MTV's *Real World 9* house, but the heart of his work is rooted most deeply in classic proportion and the vivid interplay of textures and shapes.

Ledbetter's own home proves that exquisitely. A splendid Greek Revival that rises high above the French Quarter, the 1830s townhouse reveals an artful mix of eras and influences. Originally built for a "free person of color," the structure is steeped in history and yet totally forward-looking. It boasts elaborate architectural detail and a long, lingering hallway that spills gracefully into the garden.

"I bought the house because of that hallway," Ledbetter says. "I love that you can walk in the door and glimpse the garden and have that view just pulling you forward." To take advantage of the corridor's generous size, he fashioned it as a rambling gallery space for favorite artwork. A zealous collector of contemporary photography, he's fascinated with colorful abstracts that show mundane subjects in a new light, often allowing these images to guide his décor.

In the living room, a grouping of blue-toned photos set the design scheme in motion, urging Ledbetter toward creamy ivory and pale turquoise. And in the office, where red is the primary hue, the palette was inspired by a Richard Caldicott photo featuring two surprisingly lovely Tupperware containers. "I'm definitely influenced by the artwork that I have," Ledbetter says, "but I wouldn't say it's where I start every time."

Often the furniture holds much more sway. When he and his partner, Doug Meffert, first moved in, they filled every room with mid-century modern pieces that they'd owned for years. Eventually the home's architecture encouraged a compromise. "After a few years, we just decided to tone things down," Ledbetter says. "We found several great pieces from the 1930s, and that period seemed to work really well with the neoclassical feel of the house."

Today, that balance still holds. Though much of the interior has a clean, uncluttered look and a generally "modern" vibe, it's also soft and sensual in a way that makes the space more approachable. "You can do contemporary and still have warmth," Ledbetter insists. "Honestly, I think it's nicer that way."

LEFT: In this pared-down office, a smooth Saarinen table finds the perfect texture foil in a pair of terrifically wooly draperies. Each panel is covered in showy red Koi fish, matching the tomato tone of the nearby Eames chairs.

OPPOSITE: It's all about geometry in this quiet guest bedroom, where muted walls and linens shift the focus to the shapes. Vintage sculptural lamps flank an Edward Wormley bed, with Jonathan Adler pillows and two orange line drawings adding extra oomph.

> "Miami is *in* the South, but it doesn't feel *of* the South. Design here is so fascinating because it's an international city with such a vast array of personalities."

FANNY HAIM

Living the
High Life

A vibrant tapestry of luxury high-rises spans the Miami leg of the Intracoastal Waterway, giving residents a front row seat to one of the finest maritime shows on earth. The view is phenomenal from these elegant seaside buildings, but many times, the apartments inside are not. Boxy and plain, with little variation from one to the next, they often require a skilled hand to make them beautiful and unique.

That was the challenge with this sprawling space, which designer Fanny Haim cleverly re-imagined from head to toe. Guided by the homeowners' love of Art Deco architecture—and one favorite light fixture in particular—she aimed for a modern look that was tempered with softness and warmth. Gravitating toward lush, inviting textiles and gently sweeping curves, Haim took classic contemporary furnishings and gave them just a hint of glamour.

In the bedroom, she juxtaposed the rounded shapes of a Baker bed and nightstand with the linear angles of a fabric wall. And in the living room, where a lingering row of windows spills open with sunlight, Haim fashioned a repertoire of textures and tones, playing opulent silks and linens against various wood grains and marbles.

Initially, her ultimate goal was utilitarian, with the focus of the project geared toward space planning and flow. But in the end, Haim's keen eye for color and style became the hallmark of this lavish abode. "Before coming to Miami, I was an artist in my native Colombia," she explains. "Because of this, I always view my designs through the eyes of the artist that lives inside me."

ABOVE: Fanny Haim shied away from typical Art Deco materials like zebra wood and ebony, choosing lighter toned aniegre (an African hardwood) for the shelving units in this sitting area. She also spiced up her muted ivory palette with luminous bronze draperies.

OPPOSITE: Soft cappuccino is the primary hue in this restful bedroom, where gossamer shades filter the light but not the silhouettes of the city. For added privacy and darkness, handsome woven draperies hang at the ready.

To de-emphasize the long, narrow footprint of the apartment, Jill Vantosh carved out a handful of conversation areas that are ideal for entertaining. This intimate corner of the living room is anchored by Mies van der Rohe Barcelona chairs and a modern Italian sofa.

> "One thing I've seen in the South that I haven't seen elsewhere—at least not as much—is the fact that people here *really* care about their homes."

White Hot

Jill Vantosh is often revered as Atlanta's maven of modern interiors, but the common thread in her work is certainly not contemporary style. It's art. A passionate collector who frequents dozens of shows and galleries every year, she aims to fuel that same appreciation in her clients and then create beautiful living areas around the artwork that they love.

In this home—a sleek high-rise apartment in Buckhead—Vantosh chose a bronze sculpture by artist Curt Brill as the primary focal point. Large and striking, with a playful exaggerated form, the piece draws attention but doesn't detract from the sprawling wall of windows behind. In fact, the view from the windows acts as a dreamy hued backdrop for nearly everything in the room.

Vantosh complemented the serene setting with a mostly neutral palette, using warm shades of ivory on the walls and furniture, with hints of cocoa and black. She also established an added layer of interest with lustrous chrome accents, and set the space at ease with several colorful paintings. "My goal was to create a clean, open feeling but still have a lot of warmth," Vantosh says. "Through the fabrics and the artwork and just the generally functional, comfortable flow, I really think I got it right."

What's more fitting for a home in the clouds than a little bit of sky blue? This azure-toned Egg chair and ottoman (from Fritz Hansen) soften the all-white décor and offer a quiet place to read near the cozy double fireplace.

LEFT: A skilled decorative painter, Beth Scherr created this bold "bamboo" pattern as a neutral backdrop for vibrant artwork. Her friend, Asheville artist Shelly Johnson, painted the pop art Johnny Depp image, while the bent plastic light fixture came from Italy.

OPPOSITE: A Zen influence is readily evident in this bedroom sitting area, where several Asian-style pieces meld beautifully with a clean-lined Wassily chair and a 1950s settee. Beth Scherr chose paper lanterns for the room because she liked their roundness and ethereal quality.

> "I think Southern style needs to be pleasing
> to the eye and comfortable to the soul."

True Colors

Like the pages of a well-worn diary, Beth Scherr's home tells the tale of happy days, heartbreaks, good friends, and great adventures. Serenely simple but roused by an exuberant mix of pop art and modern furniture, the 1908 Richmond rowhouse has evolved in perfect time with its owner. As Scherr's life has changed, so has her living space, giving way to a fresh, funky style that exudes happiness and warmth.

"Zen with a kick" is what she calls it, and it's quite a leap from the "Liberace meets Versace" look that she once embraced. Huge gilded frames, plush velvet, heavily carved wood—until recently, that's what Scherr preferred. But then her marriage ended and she sold her shop in Richmond's Carytown district, and suddenly her whole outlook changed. "As my life simplified, I made it a goal to simplify my surroundings too," the designer says wistfully.

Indeed, Scherr tore down walls, carved out wide open expanses, welcomed in generous waves of sunlight, and became mesmerized with the calming effects of earth tones. Wanting her home to be grounded by natural elements, she introduced equal doses of glass, metal, wood, and water into each room, and ensured that every wall color was inspired by nature. She also looked for smoother, cleaner lines in her furnishings, choosing classic modern pieces that are relatively unadorned. And as always, she eagerly incorporated her favorite found objects.

A lifelong treasure hunter, Scherr relishes the fact that she's had to search out every little knick-knack in her house. Each item has a unique story, and each, without question, is dearly loved. "I can't just rush out and buy something that everyone else has," she says. "I'm totally passionate about the hunt, even if it takes me one hundred years to find what I'm looking for. And I only buy things that really speak to me."

Scherr follows the same guidelines with her design clients, many of whom are drawn to her spirited approach and mellow demeanor. "Decorating is not supposed to be drama," she says flatly. "A lot of people find designers very intimidating because they try to lay down the law as if it's written in stone. But when I go to someone's house, I make sure it's all about them. What they love, what they feel good around, what soothes their soul and makes them happy—that's what really makes a home."

With a pale green hue on two walls and exposed brick on another, this bedroom radiates a sense of earthy tranquility. The hand-blown lamps, with shades by Jamie Young, add a dash of softness and elegance.

Offering a playful fusion of styles and cultures, the den features a pine armoire, a clean-lined ultrasuede sofa, a modern Noguchi table, and white-washed brick walls. Most of the color comes from the artwork—a mugshot painting of Ol' Blue Eyes and a woodcut print by artist Jim Dine.

Bringing Southern Style Home

ABOVE LEFT: New Country dining room collection by Ethan Allen.

ABOVE RIGHT: Oriental Toile wallpaper and fabric by Thibaut.

OPPOSITE: Emily dressing table and seat by Maine Cottage.

TRADITIONAL

Soft florals and simple styling make Lee's **3445 sofa** extra-inviting.

Carson & Co.'s cheerful **Paris lamp** brings découpaged charm to any table.

Classic toile highlights the regal lines of Ethan Allen's **Giselle chair**.

Simple **candle sconces** from French Heritage add instant ambiance.

Inlaid tulipwood gives a fresh twist to EJ Victor's **Julia Gray commode**.

Kick back and relax with the **Cherry Hill chair and ottoman** from Polmer Home Gentlemen's Quarter Collection.

Easy Elegance

Thibaut's Grace—a diminutive **wallpaper print** that complements every room.

Countless treasures can fit inside the **Arched Door bookcase** from French Heritage.

Snuggle up in style with Peacock Alley's **Vienna Matelassé bedding**.

Rejuvenation's **Hudson bowl-shade fixture** evokes the romance of yesteryear.

A traditional classic—
Ethan Allen's
Chippendale sofa.

Enjoy handcrafted beauty
with Arroyo Design's
Lorraine chair and
Neoclassic cabinet.

Wentworth **door
hardware** from
Rejuvenation
brightens any entry.

Generous tufting adds a
special touch to the **Davis
chair** from Butera Home
Furnishings.

Tailored details give
Lee's **3188 sofa** a
crisp, clean look.

Fine Lines

The **Imperial pendant fixture** from Rejuvenation invites adoring glances.

Experience woven luxury with **Empire bedding** from Gracious Style.

Carson & Co.'s turquoise **Strie lamp** is hand-painted from the inside out.

Old World elegance abounds on the **Aubusson coverlet** from Soft Surroundings.

Warm wood tones are the highlight of this **buffet** from Lexington's Liz Claiborne collection.

CASUAL

The handcrafted **Della table** from Maine Cottage has charming curves.

Ethan Allen's **New Country pie safe** holds all your home-baked goodies.

Set your rooms abloom with pretty **swirl planters** from Global Pottery.

The perfect place to curl up and read—a cozy **armchair** from the Liz Claiborne collection.

You can't help but smile in Lee's bold **214 chaise**.

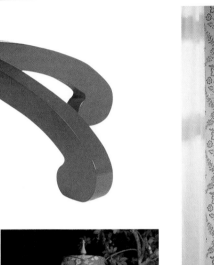

Happy Days

Broyhill's Attic Heirlooms **mirrored chest** is like a treasure passed down through the years.

The **slipcovered bed** from Lee offers softness from head to toe.

Add a dash of whimsy with the paisley-shaded **2090 lamp** from the Featherlight Lamp Company.

Lee's **3894 sofa** is simple and sweet.

Rejuvenation's **Lombard light fixture** bubbles over with retro fun.

Pale greens look pretty underfoot with Capel's **Chenango Moss rug**.

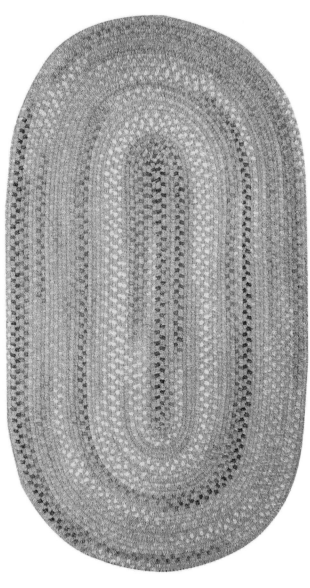

The **C3200 lamp** from Featherlight illuminates with panache.

Store your favorite silkies in Broyhill's Attic Heirlooms **lingerie chest**.

IKEA's **INGOLF armchair** exudes casual country flavor.

You're sure to have sweet dreams in the **Lizzie bed** from Maine Cottage.

Mellow Moods

Ethan Allen's New **Country corner china cabinet** features a warm, weathered finish.

Soft Surroundings' **Southampton comforter** cradles you in a cloud of comfort.

Broyhill's **Fliptop console** brings quick-change convenience to any room.

Topiary wallpaper from Thibaut's Canterbury collection welcomes the outdoors in.

Easy does it with the chunky **dining table** from Maine Cottage.

GETTING THE LOOK RUSTIC

Handsome carved legs hold up Broyhill's **upholstered back chair.**

Mexican Serape bedding from the Chandler Collection evokes a simpler time.

A colorful mélange of antique images adorns Carson & Co.'s **Black Forest chest.**

Heathered wool lends added dimension to Garnet Hill's vibrant **Sierra Valley rug.**

Natural Wonders

Enjoy a bit of Asian flair with PierceMartin's **Bronze Rangoon table**.

Savor the suppleness of Butera Home Furnishings' **Grant chair**.

The warm glow of Rejuvenation's **Pearl fixture** is like no other.

Jonathan Adler's **Relief pottery** illustrates the appeal of organic shapes.

A festive array of fabrics ornaments the **Jewel sofa** from EJ Victor's Carol Bolton collection.

Butera's **Somerset sofa** boasts antique casters and double-turned legs.

Simplicity becomes stunning with Arroyo Design's **tapered-leg dining table** and Lorraine chairs.

The cozy **1708 armchair** from Lee offers a supremely soft place to fall.

EJ Victor's **Bunchable étagère** offers two tiers of display space.

Amazing embroidery embellishes the Chandler Collection's **Spanish folk art bedding**.

An artful pattern of garden glories covers Capel's **Nepal Passage rug**.

Fireside Favorites

Galbraith & Paul's **Funnel pendants** deliver hand-printed perfection.

Classic Eastlake motifs are the hallmark of Rejuvenation's **Edwards door hardware**.

Woven wicker forms the base of Lexington's **Smithsonian Museum chair and ottoman**.

The **Colton sconce** from Rejuvenation glimmers with three smoky glass panels.

Lee's divinely soft **3010 sofa** brings new meaning to rustic style.

Cascading vines cover nearly every inch of the Chandler Collection's **Philippine Lace bedding**.

A bounty of seashells bejewels Carson & Co.'s framed **Grotto prints**.

Discover the ageless elegance of **Venini's Incisi vases**.

The large **Turk lamp** from Tracy Glover Studio is a hand-blown work of art.

Zebra stripes add a spark to Lee's **521 ottoman**.

Breezy Blues

Take the patchwork plunge with InterfaceFLOR's **Thick & Thin, House Pet, and Fast Forward tiles.**

You can't resist the whimsical shapes of Hable Construction's wool felt pillows.

With Peacock Alley's **Miramar Steel bedding,** quilted softness never felt so good.

Clean lines and cushy too—that's the beauty of **Lee's 801 chaise.**

All eyes are drawn to the turquoise finish on French Heritage's **Regence Style commode.**

The **Gramercy chair** from Butera Home Furnishings is ideal for entertaining.

Lazy days are made for the **metal scroll bed** from Lexington's Liz Claiborne collection.

Swirls of needlepoint sashay playfully across Garnet Hill's **Vortex quilt**.

You'll see the finest flora and fauna on the **Highlands lamp** from Carson & Co.

Fall in love with the unique charm of Carson & Co.'s **Black Forest cabinet**.

Ravishing Reds

InterfaceFLOR's interchangeable **House Pet tiles** are the squares beyond compare.

Simplicity at its finest— **IKEA's MURAN armchair.**

Shimmering silk meets marvelous metallic on Michele Varian's **metal rose pillows**.

The **Humboldt hanging fixture** from Rejuvenation offers just the light you need.

It's all about the fabric on Lee's sublime **2290 sofa**.

Minka Aire's **Cirque fan** from G Squared offers a creative take on airflow.

Connect the dots with Chiasso's **Chocolate Circles bedding**.

Discover lilac bliss with Hable Construction's quirky **wool felt pillows**.

Nab the long and lean **Flos spun lamp** at **SPACE**.

The **Angelis chair** from Dunbar Furniture takes an angular approach to comfort.

Seductive Shapes

Heavenly curves made Modernica's **Cloud sofa** irresistible.

Hand-blown beads form the base of the **Susan lamp** from Tracy Glover Studio.

When ordinary pillows just won't do, rest your head on Intoto's **Billows**.

Kartell's **Prince AHA stools** are excellent for seating and serving.

The **FRIDENE chair** from IKEA hugs your body like a glove.

The **Tug Boat sectional** from In House Furniture is sure to spark good conversation.

Before Heller's **Arco Bellini chair**, who knew plastic could be so cool?

Color your world with Venini's Quattro Stagioni **art glass sculpture**.

Brighten your life with the unique ceramic form of the **Double Stack egg lamp**.

A simple shape becomes super useful with IKEA's eight-drawer **ROBIN chest**.

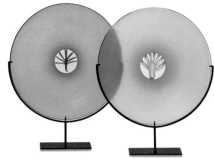

Colors collide beautifully with **Solid Ground tiles** from InterfaceFLOR.

You'll chat for hours in the **Tête-à-Tête sofa** from Dunbar Furniture.

Radiant Retro

Antique patterns get a modern twist with Jonathan Adler's **needlepoint pillows**.

A vintage classic is revived with Modernica's **stacking shell chairs**.

Discover the new shape of storage with In House Furniture's **Circle 3 magazine table**.

The streamlined look lingers on with Rejuvenation's **Trenton pendant light**.

A diminutive little darling—the **Otis sofa** from Maine Cottage.

DESIGNER DIRECTORY

Joan Brendle
Laurel Park, NC
USA
828.694.0299

Sonia Cruz de Baltodano
Delphi Architects & Town Planners
60 Casuarina Concourse
Miami, FL 33143
USA
786.268.8017

Gretchen Edwards
Gilstrap Edwards Interior Design
345 Peachtree Hills Avenue NE
Atlanta, GA 30305
USA
404.869.4401
www.gilstrapedwards.com

Gloria Frame
Houston, TX
USA
713.681.9996

Gwynn Griffith
San Antonio, TX
USA
210.534.0818

Kathy Guyton
Guyton Design Group, Inc.
349 Peachtree Hills Avenue NE
Atlanta, GA 30305
USA
404.995.0000

Fanny Haim
Fanny Haim & Associates
21338 West Dixie Highway
Miami, FL 33180
USA
305.937.0815
www.fannyhaim.com

Brooke Huttig
Kemble Interiors
294 Hibiscus Avenue
Palm Beach, FL 33480
USA
561.659.5556
www.kembleinteriors.com

Suzanne Kasler
Suzanne Kasler Interiors
2300 Peachtree Road NW
Atlanta, GA 30309
USA
404.355.1035
www.suzannekasler.com

Jackye Lanham
Jacquelynne P. Lanham & Associates
472 East Paces Ferry Road NE
Atlanta, GA 30305
USA
404.364.0472

Lee Ledbetter
Lee Ledbetter Architects
1055 St. Charles Avenue
Suite 320
New Orleans, LA 70130
USA
504.566.9669
www.leeledbetter.com

Candy Lloyd
Candler Lloyd Interiors
349 Peachtree Hills Avenue NE
Atlanta, GA 30305
USA
404.237.8606
www.candlerlloyd.com

Susan Massey
Bohlert-Massey Interiors
35 Clayton Lane
Santa Rosa Beach, FL 32459
USA
850.231.3940

Mimi McMakin
Kemble Interiors
294 Hibiscus Avenue
Palm Beach, FL 33480
USA
561.659.5556
www.kembleinteriors.com

Rod Mickley
Rod Mickley Interior Design
3001 Ocean Drive
Suite 201
Vero Beach, FL 32963
USA
772.234.4550
www.rodmickley.com

Joseph Minton
1410 Slocum Street
Dallas, TX 75207
USA
214.744.3111
www.mintonantiques.com

Helaine Moyse
Helaine Moyse Interior Design
2974 Reymond Avenue
Baton Rouge, LA 70808
USA
225.344.9778

Mike Ruegamer
Group 3 Architecture Interiors Planning
1600 Main Street
Hilton Head, SC 29926
USA
843.689.9060
www.group3arch.com

Tim Schelfe
Steiner + Schelfe Design
1838 Wake Forest Road
Raleigh, NC 27618
USA
919.832.8323
www.steinerschelfe.com

Beth Scherr
Richmond, VA
USA
804.354.9939

Lisa Sherry
High Point, NC
USA
336.688.2483

Phillip Sides
104 North Barrett Square
Rosemary Beach, FL 32461
USA
850.231.5380
www.phillipsidesinteriordesign.com

Jim Smith
Dixon Smith Interiors
1655 Lobdell Avenue
Baton Rouge, LA 70806
USA
225.927.4261
www.dixonsmithinteriors.com

Michael Steiner
Steiner + Schelfe Design
1838 Wake Forest Road
Raleigh, NC 27618
USA
919.832.8323
www.steinerschelfe.com

Bill Stewart
William Stewart Designs
349 Peachtree Hills Avenue NE
Atlanta, GA 30305
USA
404.816.2501

Jon Vaccari
Jon Vaccari Design
4858 Magazine Street
New Orleans, LA 70115
USA
504.899.7632
www.jonvaccaridesign.com

Jill Vantosh
Vantosh and Associates
1473 Spring Street NW
Atlanta, GA 30309
USA
404.888.0613

Babs Watkins
Babs Watkins Design
2314 Bissonnet Street
Houston, TX 77005
USA
713.529.5428

Eric Watson
2909 West Bay to Bay Boulevard
Suite 206
Tampa, FL 33629
USA
813.835.7595
www.ericwatson.com

Peggy Westerman
Baton Rouge, LA
USA
225.927.5233
www.bienvillequarters.com

Artists & Architects

William T. Baker, *architect*
404.261.0446
www.wtbaker.com

Curt Brill, *sculptor*
520.888.1775
www.curtbrill.com

Richard Caldicott, *photographer*
www.richardcaldicott.co.uk

Lisa diStefano, *painter*
225.927.767
www.annconnelly.com

Lawrence Gipe, *painter*
www.lawrencegipe.com

Jay Iarussi, *decorative painter*
832.419.3014

Shelly M. Johnson, *painter*
828.254.6013
www.smjdesigns.us

Kenward Architectural Studio
404.603.9191
www.kenward.com

Julio Larraz, *painter*
www.juliolarraz.net

Don B. McDonald, *architect*
210.735.9722

Yong Pak, *architect*
404.231.3195
www.pakheydt.com

Hunt Slonem, *painter*
212.620.4835
www.huntslonem.com

Brad Stephens, *artist/craftsman*
804.438.5350

Shops & Sources

Arroyo Design
520.884.1012
www.arroyo-design.com

Baker Furniture
800.59.BAKER
www.kohlerinteriors.com

Butera Home Furnishings
949.650.8570
www.barclaybutera.com

Broyhill Furniture Industries, Inc.
800.3.BROYHILL
www.broyhillfurn.com

Brunschwig & Fils
914.684.5800
www.brunschwig.com

Capel
800.382.6574
www.capelrugs.com

Carson & Co.
704.332.5955
www.carsonandco.com

Chiasso
877.244.2776
www.chiasso.com

Chandler Collection
323.266.8993
www.thechandlercollection.com

Creation Baumann
www.creationbaumann.com

Dessin Fournir
785.434.2777
www.dessinfournir.com

Dunbar Furniture
336.734.1700
www.collectdunbar.com

Egg Lamps
866.EGG.LAMP
www.egglamp.com

EJ Victor
828.437.1991
www.ejvictor.com

Ethan Allen
888.EAHELP.1
www.ethanallen.com

Featherlight Lamp Company
www.featherlightlamp.com

Fortuny
212.753.7153
www.fortuny.com

French Heritage
800.245.0899
www.frenchheritage.com

Fritz Hansen
646.495.6183
www.fritzhansen.com

Galbraith & Paul
215.508.0800
www.galbraithandpaul.com

Garnet Hill
800.870.3513
www.garnethill.com

Global Pottery
631.694.8100
www.globalpottery.com

Gracious Style
888.828.7170
www.graciousstyle.com

G Squared
877.858.5333
www.g2art.com

Hable Construction
877.HABLE.04
www.hableconstruction.com

Heller
212.685.4200
www.helleronline.com

IKEA
800.434.4532
www.ikea.com

In House Furniture
323.655.2116
www.inhousefurniture.com

InterfaceFLOR
866.281.FLOR
www.interfaceflor.com

Intoto
917.671.7923
www.intotonyc.com

Jamie Young Company
866.29.LAMPS
www.jamieyoung.com

Jonathan Adler
877.287.1910
www.jonathanadler.com

Kartell
212.625.1494
www.kartell.com

Kravet Fabrics
800.648.5728
www.kravet.com

Larsen (Cowtan & Tout)
212.627.7878

Lee Industries
800.892.7150
www.leeindustries.com

Lexington Home Brands
800.LEX.INFO
www.lexington.com

Liz Claiborne
866.549.7467
www.lizclaiborne.com

Longstreet Collection
314.961.3382
www.longstreetcollection.com

Maine Cottage
888.859.5522
www.mainecottage.com

Maitland-Smith
336.812.2400
www.maitland-smith.com

Michele Varian
212.343.0033
www.michelevarian.com

Mike Bell
312.644.6848
www.mikebellonline.com

Minton-Corley Collection
817.332.3111

Modernica
323.933.0383
www.modernica.net

Palmer Home
800.LEX.INFO
www.lexington.com

Peacock Alley
800.652.3818
www.peacockalley.com

Phillip & Co
850.267.1987
www.phillipandco.com

PierceMartin
800.334.8701
www.piercemartin.com

Ralph Lauren
888.475.7674
www.polo.com

Raoul Textiles
805.965.1694
www.raoultextiles.com

Rejuvenation
888.401.1900
www.rejuvenation.com

Rogers & Goffigon Ltd.
212.888.3242

Rose Tarlow
323.651.2202
www.rosetarlow.com

Saladino Furniture
212.684.3720
www.saladinofurniture.com

Soft Surroundings
800.749.7638
www.softsurroundings.com

SPACE
404.228.4600
www.spacemodern.com

Stark Carpet Corporation
212.752.9000
www.starkcarpet.com

Thibaut
800.223.0704
www.thibautdesign.com

Tracy Glover Studio
401.461.1560
www.tracygloverstudio.com

Travers
212.888.7900
www.traversinc.com

Venini
212.696.9640
www.venini.it

Watkins Culver
713.529.0597

ABOUT THE AUTHOR

Shannon Howard is a writer and scout for an eclectic array of interior design magazines, both in the U.S. and abroad. Her company, Colossal Creative, is based in St. Louis.

ACKNOWLEDGMENTS

This book is a testament to the talent and kindness of more than two dozen interior designers, all of whom graciously shared their unique insights on work, style, and life. Their colorful stories and vibrant personalities set the tone for this project, making it a joy to work on and an experience to treasure.

Special thanks to Rockport's Mary Ann Hall, whose tremendous faith got the book up and running, and who, despite being wearily close to her due date, continued to offer stellar advice and guidance. Her vision was instrumental throughout, lending direction and focus even from afar.

My deepest gratitude to Rockport's Betsy Gammons for being a brave and faithful companion on this great adventure. Besides tracking down countless photos and smoothing over myriad snags, she was a patient teacher, a voice of reason, and an always-dependable source of laughter and levity. Without her creativity and uncompromising commitment to quality, this project wouldn't have been the same.

Finally, much love to my husband, Keith, who generously endured months of frenzied writing and early-morning deliveries while *Southern Rooms* was in progress. Thank you for always being, as Dr. Phil calls it, "a soft place to fall."

PHOTOGRAPHER CREDITS

Paul Bardagjy/Through the Lens Management
71 (top right); 72; 73; 74; 75; 82; 83; 84; 85

Antoine Bootz
39 (top right); 66; 67; 68; 69

Courtesy of the Chandler Collection
71 (bottom)

Courtesy of Chiasso
115 (top left)

Davies & Lawery
70

Carlos Domenech
60; 61; 102; 103; 104; 105; 114; 120; 121

Courtesy of French Heritage
7 (right); 11 (left)

Tony Giammarino/Giammarino & Dworkin
54; 55; 62; 63; 64; 65; 124; 125; 126; 127

Tria Giovan
26; 27; 28; 29; 30; 31; 56; 57; 58; 59; 110; 111; 112; 113

Steve Gross & Susan Daley
76; 77; 78; 79

John M. Hall
14; 15; 19

Chipper Hatter
34; 35; 80; 81; 98; 99

Courtesy of InterfaceFLOR
115 (bottom)

Mark Knight
20

Courtesy of Rod Mickley Interior Design/www.rodmickley.com
90

Emily Minton-Redfield
9; 48; 49; 86; 87; 88; 89; 100; 101; 122; 123

Courtesy of Peacock Alley
11 (right)

Courtesy of PierceMartin
7 (left); 71 (top left)

Richard Sexton
12; 16; 17; 108; 109; 115 (top right); 116; 117; 118; 119

Courtesy of Thibaut
6; 10

Seth Tice-Lewis
8; 21 (bottom); 32; 33

Eugenia Uhl
94; 95; 96; 97

Brian Vanden Brink
18; 50; 51; 52; 53

Andreas von Einsiedel
40; 41; 42; 43

William Waldron
21 (top); 22; 23; 24; 25

Deborah Whitlaw
36; 37; 92; 93

Ted Yarwood
5; 38; 39 (top left & bottom); 44; 45; 46; 47; 91; 106; 107